To: Jake Lee O'Connor
on your Christening Day
October 21, 2001

God Bless you always.

Love,
"Auntie" Reenie
xoxo

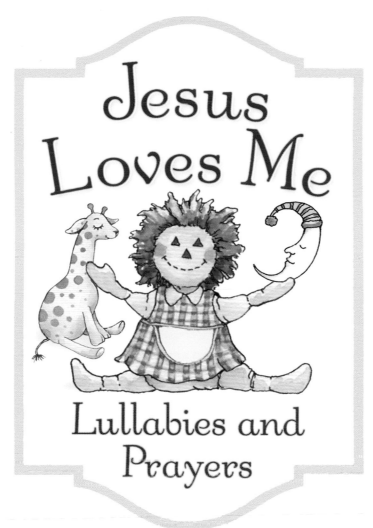

Jesus Loves Me

Lullabies and Prayers

Poems by
HELEN HAIDLE

Illustrations by
DAVID HAIDLE & ELIZABETH HAIDLE

HARVEST
HOUSE
PUBLISHERS

Eugene, Oregon 97402

To all Fathers, Mothers, Grandparents, and Caregivers,
Who tuck God's precious children in bed—
Be encouraged! God promises to richly bless the seeds you plant.

And to
Jeannie Taylor and Barbara Martin,
Who generously pray, encourage, and critique.
They've also planted seeds in this treasury of poems.

Jesus Loves Me Lullabies and Prayers
Formerly Sleepy-Time Rhymes
Copyright © 1998 Helen Haidle
Illustrations copyright © 1998 David Haidle and Elizabeth Haidle
Book design by Terry Dugan, Mpls. MN
Published by Harvest House Publishers
Eugene, Oregon 97402

Library of Congress Cataloging-in-Publication Data
Haidle, Helen
  [Sleepy-time rhymes for little ones]
  Jesus loves me lullabies & prayers / text by Helen Haidle ; illustrations by David Haidle & Elizabeth Haidle.
    p.cm.
  ISBN 0-7369-0197-3
    1. Lullabies, American. 2. Children's poetry, American. 3. Christian poetry, American.
  [1. Lullabies. 2. Christian life—Poetry. 3. American poetry.] I. Title: Jesus loves me lullabies and prayers. II. Haidle, David, ill. III. Haidle, Elizabeth, 1974-ill. IV. Title.

  PS3558.A3247 S56 2001
  811'.54—dc21   00-047122

Unless otherwise indicated, Scripture quotations are from the Contemporary English Version, Copyright © 1995 American Bible Society. Published by Thomas Nelson, Inc., Publishers. Used by permission. Verses marked NKJ are taken from the New King James Version, Copyright © 1979, 1980, 1982 by Thomas Nelson, Inc., Publishers. Used by permission. Verses marked NIV are taken from the Holy Bible, New International Version®. Copyright © 1973, 1978, 1984 by the International Bible Society. Used by permission of Zondervan Publishing House.

Printed in Hong Kong.
01 02 03 04 05 06 07 08 09 10 /IM/ 10 9 8 7 6 5 4 3 2 1

Dear Families,

Many ideas in this book began over 20 years ago when we sought God's guidance to help our children through troubles, sickness, worries, fears of the dark, etc. When nightmares bothered Jonathan, our firstborn, we found that the assurance of God's presence, reminders of God's faithful promises, and prayer—placing worry and fear in God's hands—helped dispel the bad dreams. We discovered that praise and singing lifted our spirits and put a song in our hearts.

Although we've never had "material" wealth to give our children, we've shared with them a richer heritage...from God. Looking back, we see that times together with them and with God were more precious and important than we realized.

Bedtime became an important time together. Reading the Bible and other books was always a nightly ritual. Afterward, we helped "fly" them to bed (until they were too heavy to carry!). We sang and prayed in their rooms, then gave back rubs as we spent extra time blessing them and singing. (Paul, our youngest, still asks for a back rub and song when he comes home on college breaks!)

Even when they were little, our children knew it meant something special when our finger "drew" a cross on their foreheads and blessed them. At less than one year old, Elizabeth would pull our fingers to her forehead and wait for us to pray.

You, too, can lay the foundation for your child's lasting relationship with God. Ask God for help in making bedtime an opportunity to draw close to Him and to each other. Kneel by your children's beds as you pray and bless them. Sing to your children—don't worry if you can't carry a tune. "Joyful noise" delights the Lord, so use the voice you have.

Taking time to sow seeds of God's Word and Love is worth every effort. Now we see the end result—the fruit—of what we planted these past 24 years. And nothing surpasses the joy of seeing our grown children walk with God and serve others.

We are pleased to share with you some things we found to be important with our kids. Be assured: Your children, too, will trust God and love others...just plant those seeds! God is the One who brings forth the "harvest."

God bless you and your little ones,

David and Helen

Where Do Babies Sleep?

a poem

Oh, where do babies fall asleep?

Where do they lay their heads?

The baby colt and filly

Lie down on straw for beds.

The piglets sleep in pigsties,
While calves sleep in the barn.
The oxen sleep in stables,
And cats curl up with yarn.

But what about the insects,
Like bees and ladybugs?
Do they get wrapped in blankets,
With kisses, pats, and hugs?

I'm glad I have a blankie.
I'm thankful for my bed,
My family's love and kisses,
And pats upon my head.

Tell the LORD how thankful you are.
PSALM 118:1

5

In His Hands

(Tune: "*He's Got the Whole World In His Hands*")

He's got the mamas and the babies in His hands.

He's got the mamas and the babies in His hands.

He's got the mamas and the babies in His hands.

He's got the whole world in His hands.

♥ ♥ ♥ ♥ ♥

Jesus said,
*"My sheep know my voice, and I know them…No one
can snatch them out of my hand."*
JOHN 10:27,28

(Slowly and quietly)

He's got the sleepy little children in His hands.

He's got the sleepy little children in His hands.

He's got the sleepy little children in His hands.

He's got the whole world in His hands.

♥ ♥ ♥ ♥ ♥

God says,

"Since the day you were born, I have carried you…
I will carry you and always keep you safe."

ISAIAH 46:3,4

My Sleepy Fingers

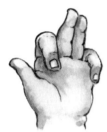

*I*t's time for sleepy fingers
To snuggle down in bed.
First you, my Baby Finger,
Tuck in your drowsy head.
It's bedtime, Mister Ring Man,
With your friend, Tall Man great.
Please hurry, Pointer Finger.
It's getting mighty late!
Is every finger cozy?
Oh, no! There's one to come—
Move over, Pointer Finger,
Here comes my
Busy Thumb!

Good Night, World!

Every wild and tame animal, all reptiles and birds, come praise the LORD.
PSALM 148:10

Good night,

Dear cats and puppy dogs.

Good night,

Small birds and croaking frogs.

Good night,

To bugs and honeybees,

To butterflies

And chickadees.

Good night,

To all whose voices raise

Loud barks and chirps

To give God praise!

God Loves Me Always

(Tune: *"My Bonnie Lies Over the Ocean"*)

God's love is as deep as the ocean.

God's love is as high as the sky.

God's love overflows all around me;

There's no need to worry or cry.

CHORUS

Love me, always;

God promised to always

Love me, love me.

Love me, always;

God promised to always love me.

◇   ◇   ◇   ◇   ◇

How great is God's love for all who worship him?
Greater than the distance between heaven and earth!

PSALM 103:11

Come look at the beautiful roses.

God gave them bright petals to wear.

They smile at the sun and look pretty.

They don't have a worry or care.

CHORUS

Love me, always;

God promised to always

Love me, love me.

Love me, always;

God promised to always love me.

Jesus said,
"Look how the wild flowers grow!...
God gives such beauty to everything that grows in the field...
won't he do even more for you?"
LUKE 12:27,28

God cares for the robin and blue jay.

God sees when they fall from their nest.

God tells me that I'm more important;

Now safe in His love, I can rest.

CHORUS

Love me, always;

God promised to always

Love me, love me.

Love me, always;

God promised to always love me.

✧   ✧   ✧   ✧

Jesus said,
*"God takes care of [the birds].
And you are much more important than any birds."*
L U K E   1 2 : 2 2 - 2 4

God Is Good

The golden sun sets in the west,
As stars begin to shine.
The birds sleep silent in their nest;
Now I must sleep in mine.

I thank You, God, for stars and rain,
And for my cozy bed,
For rainbow skies and daisy chains,
For milk and gingerbread.

*With all my heart I praise the LORD! I will never
forget how kind he has been.*
PSALM 103:2

I Love You!

a poem...

I love you much more
Than frogs love to catch flies,
Or ants love a picnic
And strawberry pies.

♥

I love you much more
Than mice love to eat cheese,
Or birds love to nest
In the old apple trees.

We love because God loved us first.
1 JOHN 4:19

I love you much more
Than a cat loves to purr,
Or bunnies love snuggling
In mother's soft fur.

♥

I love you much more
Than the stars love to shine.
I'll love you forever,
Dear baby of mine!

A Penguin Lullaby

Let every living creature praise the LORD.
PSALM 150:6

Way down in Antarctic, where freezing wind blows,
A brave penguin dad holds an egg on his toes.

a poem

Oh hush,

My Egg-Baby.

Please sleep now and rest.

I wish I could build you

A warm, cozy nest.

You won't crack or freeze

If you rest on my toes.

I'll stand still and hold you;

I'll patiently doze.

I won't eat or drink.

I'll wait sixty long days.

And when you crack open,

I'll give God

The praise!"

16

God Cares for Me

(Tune: *"Jesus Loves Me"*)

God feeds the baby birds so small;

Watches when they faint or fall.

God takes such good care of me.

God's dear child, I'll always be.

CHORUS

God feeds the sparrows.

God feeds the sparrows.

God feeds the sparrows.

I know God cares for me.

Jesus said,

*"So don't be afraid; you are worth much
more than many sparrows."*

MATTHEW 10:31 NIV

Night Song

(Tune: *"Sing a Song of Sixpence"*)

Sing of God's creation,

Of all the stars so bright.

Sing while flick'ring fireflies

Light the darkest night.

Watch for falling stars

That disappear from sight.

Sleep and dream of windy days

When you can fly a kite.

★ ★ ★ ★ ★

Praise the LORD...Tell everyone what he has done.
Sing praises to the LORD
PSALM 105:1, 2

See the baby robins,

Who snuggle in their nest,

Cuddling close to mother,

Trying to take a rest.

Watch the blazing sunset

Lighting up the West.

When it's growing dark, you'll hear

The frogs who *croak* their best!

Your Stuffed Friends

Please pick up all your stuffed friends,
And pile them on your bed.

Bring Pooh and Peter Rabbit,
A funny frog named Fred.

Bring ladybug and pet rocks
We found behind the shed.

Then wink Good-night,
And squeeze them tight,
You happy Sleepyhead!

Be glad that you belong to the Lord.
PHILIPPIANS 3:1

20

Sleep and Dream

Sleep and dream,
My precious Baby.
Snuggle down
And take your rest.

Float across the
Dreamland River,
Cuddled in
Your cozy nest.

♥ ♥ ♥

a poem...

The Smells of Night

Let's smell the night air and the bubbling brooks,
And sweet pastry odors from late midnight cooks.

The early-bird bakers mix batches of bread,
And soon, from the oven, smells drift overhead.

Thank God for your nose and the smells in the sky,
Of lilacs and roses and sweet cherry pie.

✧ ✧ ✧ ✧

God...blesses us with everything we need to enjoy life.
1 TIMOTHY 6:17

22

I Love Jesus

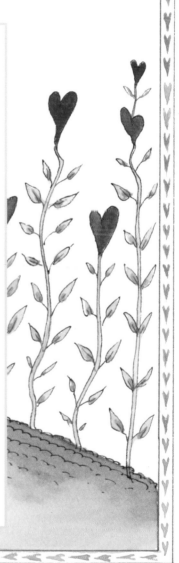

(Tune: *"Jesus Loves Me"*)

I love Jesus. Does He know?

Do I ever tell Him so?

Jesus wants to hear me say

That I love Him every day.

CHORUS

Jesus, I love You!

Jesus, I love You!

Jesus, I love You!

Because You first loved me.

♥ ♥ ♥ ♥ ♥

Jesus said,
"I love you, just as my Father has loved me."

JOHN 15:9

In the Treetops

(Tune: *"Rock-a-bye Baby"*)

Rock-a-bye, baby, in the treetop.

When the wind blows, your cradle will rock.

Smell the sweet blossoms, sway in the trees,

And swing in the branches blown by the breeze.

Rock-a-bye baby, lie down to sleep.

Rest on a flower, snuggle in deep.

Watch baby spiders learning to spin,

While robins build nests in treetops again.

* * * * *

God takes care of his own, even while they sleep.
PSALM 127:2

Rock-a-bye, baby, how I love you.

You're my sweet gift from Heaven, 'tis true!

Angels surround you, keep you from harm,

While God holds you safely—rest in His arm.

The eternal God...carries us in his arms.
DEUTERONOMY 33:27

How to Fall Asleep

First close your left eye,

Now your right.

Shut them both together,

And hold them tight.

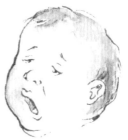

Then sneak a quick peek,

Silently.

Through your narrowed eyes,

You can barely see.

Oh, take a big breath,

Long and deep.

Say a little prayer,

And fall fast asleep!

Rest in the LORD.
PSALM 37:7 NKJ

27

God's Blessing

I'll give you God's blessing as you go to bed,
By laying my hands on your sweet, precious head.

You're God's own dear child, and I pray you are blest.
Lean back on your pillow; in peace may you rest.

*The LORD bless you! I give you my blessing
in the name of the LORD.*
PSALM 129:8

Angels All Around

For [God] will give His angels charge over you
to keep you in all your ways.

PSALM 91:11 NKJ

(Tune: *"Jesus Loves Me"*)

God sends angels I can't see.

They are watching over me,

Standing by my feet and head,

Angels all around my bed.

CHORUS

God sends His angels.

God sends His angels.

God sends His angels

To guard and care for me.

Hugs and Tickles

My hugs and pats and kisses, and tiny tickles, too,

Are little ways of showing how much I care for you!

I'll wrap you up in blankets and squeeze you oh-so-tight.

Your ears will hear me whisper,

"Sweet dreams all through the night!"

♥ ♥ ♥ ♥ ♥

*If we love each other, God lives in us and his
love is truly in our hearts.*

1 JOHN 4:12

As You Fall Asleep

I will praise you, LORD, with all my heart.
PSALM 9:1

When you fall asleep tonight,

Count the evening stars so bright,

As they sparkle in the sky,

While the puffy clouds float by.

See the glowing moon appear

In the purple sky so clear.

Smell the sweet perfume of Spring;

Thank the Lord, give praise to Him.

Peaceful Night

(Tune: *"The Wheels on the Bus"*)

The stars in the sky will twinkle bright,

Twinkle bright, twinkle bright.

The stars in the sky will twinkle bright—

All through the night.

[God] decided how many stars there would be in the sky
and gave each one a name.

PSALM 147:4

The children in bed are tucked in tight,

Tucked in tight, tucked in tight.

The children in bed are tucked in tight—

All through the night.

* * * * *

You, LORD, are the light that keeps me safe.
I am not afraid of anyone. You protect me,
and I have no fears.

PSALM 27:1

Your Little Garden

There is a garden growing,
Right there inside your heart.
And every time you hear God's Word,
A good seed gets its start.

Take time to think of God's dear Son;
That's planting seeds of Love.
Remember all He's done for you.
He came from Heav'n above.

Please think of all that's beautiful—
Right, honest, pure, and fair.
Plant seeds of good deeds in your home
With sharing, love, and prayer.

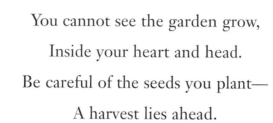

You cannot see the garden grow,
Inside your heart and head.
Be careful of the seeds you plant—
A harvest lies ahead.

If you neglect to plant God's seeds,
Then *weeds* begin to grow.
But if you pray and trust in God,
Those are good seeds you sow.

Before you fall asleep tonight,
Let's plant some little seeds.
We'll read the Bible, God's own Word,
And thank God for His deeds.

❁ ❁ ❁ ❁ ❁

Keep your minds on whatever is true, pure,
right, holy, friendly, and proper.
PHILIPPIANS 4:8

productive fruit…

a basket-full of Blessings…

Bedtime Countdown

*O*ne, two—

    Take off your shoe.

Three, four—

    Better not snore!

Five, six—

    Stop pulling tricks!

Seven, eight—

    It's getting late!

Nine, ten—

    Bedtime again!

God Cares for You

Let's give God our worries, our fears, and our cares.

We surely can trust Him; He's counted our hairs!

So don't be afraid as I sing o'er your bed,

For angels of God keep their watch overhead.

♥ ♥ ♥ ♥ ♥

Even the hairs on your head are counted. So don't be afraid!
MATTHEW 10:30,31

When I Feel Afraid

When I feel afraid in bed,

Is God watching overhead?

Pull the covers over me—

When I'm hiding, can God see?

⋄ ⋄ ⋄ ⋄ ⋄

*I am the LORD your God. I am holding your hand,
so don't be afraid. I am here to help you.*

ISAIAH 41:13

In the Dark

(Tune: *"Jesus Loves Me"*)

When it's dark and I can't see,

God still watches over me.

Darkness is the same as light;

God sees clearly in the night.

CHORUS

Yes, God can see me.

Yes, God can see me.

Yes, God can see me.

God sees me in the dark.

*[God], you see in the dark because daylight and dark
are all the same to you.*

PSALM 139:12

A Day with Daddy

*P*lay with your daddy, my little laddie,

Play with your daddy, my little man.

Skip through the waves and peer in the caves,

Run through the ripples in the golden sand.

❤ ❤ ❤ ❤ ❤

Love is more important than anything else.
COLOSSIANS 3:14

Sing with your daddy, my little laddie,

Sing with your daddy, my little man.

Under the moon, let's whistle a tune;

Lie on a blanket in the golden sand.

Pray with your daddy, my little laddie,

Pray with your daddy, my little man.

Count stars above. Thank God for His love.

Camp on the beaches full of golden sand.

♥ ♥ ♥ ♥ ♥

God Most High, I will rejoice; I will celebrate
and sing because of you.
PSALM 9:2

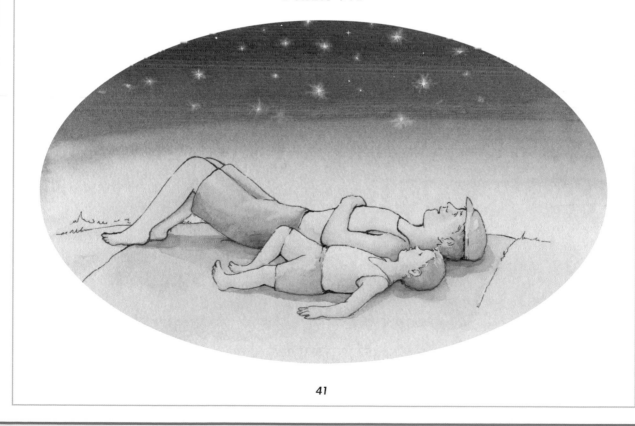

Time for Bed

Please tippy-toe softly
To your bedroom door;
Pull out your pajamas
From inside your drawer.

A warm, snuggly nightcap
Fits over your head;
While Grandma's wool quilt
Keeps you cozy in bed.

Wave *night-night* to Jesus.
He sees all you do.
He won't fall asleep
While He's caring for you.

❀ ❀ ❀ ❀

The Lord...won't go to sleep.
PSALM 121:3

Recipe for Sweet Dreams

Start with one big snuggly hug;

Add a pinch or two of love.

Plant a kiss on each round cheek,

Little ears so gently tweak.

With your fingers, gently scratch

Shoulders, neck, and 'round the back.

✧ ✧ ✧ ✧ ✧

*God wants us to have faith in his Son Jesus Christ
and to love each other.*

1 JOHN 3:23

Watch the Colors!

God gives the gift of sunshine
To color up each day.
But later, in the evening,
The sunshine slips away.

Then cheerful daylight colors
Turn into shades of gray,
Then darken into blackest night
As colors fade away.

Our clothes lose all their dots and stripes;

Blue, yellow, red, and pink.

The trees and grass lose all their green,

They look like blobs of ink!

The gentle glow of moonlight

Spreads shadows on the lawn.

But God will bring the colors back,

When the sun appears at dawn.

★ ★ ★ ★ ★

I am the LORD God. I created the heavens...
the earth and everything...on it.
ISAIAH 42:5

45

God Loves Your Tummy-Tum

God loves your tummy-tum.

(Blow on tummy)

God loves your turned-up nose.

(Rub noses)

God loves your boney ribs

(Tickle ribs)

And all your wiggly toes.

(Run fingers over toes)

(Repeat, using: "I love...")

♥ ♥ ♥ ♥ ♥

God is love...
We love because God loved us first.
1 John 4:17,19

God's Great Love

(Tune: "Jesus Loves Me")

God's love reaches very high,
Far beyond the clear blue sky.
Look up in the starry night;
God's love stretches out of sight.

CHORUS

God's love is bigger.
God's love is bigger.
God's love is bigger
And higher than the sky.

★ ★ ★ ★ ★

*As high as the heavens are above the earth,
so great is [God's] love.*
PSALM 103:11 NIV

47

Who's Going to Bed?

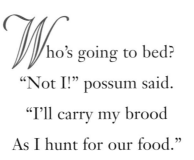

Who's going to bed?

"Not I!" possum said.

"I'll carry my brood

As I hunt for our food."

Who's going to snore?

"Not I!" said the boar.

"Perhaps a slight moan

Or a squeal or a groan."

★ ★ ★ ★ ★

Who wanders at night?
Cat grinned with delight.
"I slept through the day,
And now I want to play!"

Who's going to sleep?
"We are," said the sheep.
"In coldest of weather,
We snuggle together."

Who's going to pray
At the close of the day?
"We will," children said,
As they knelt by their bed.

★ ★ ★ ★ ★

Dear Jesus

Dear Jesus,
I thank You for fam'ly,
And good food to eat,
For kittens and puppies,
And shoes on my feet.

I thank You for helping me
Grow and be strong,
Through times of great trouble,
When things go all wrong.

Please stay close beside me
Through every dark night,
And make my heart happy
With sun's morning light."
Amen.

*You have been good
to me, LORD,
and I will sing about you.*
PSALM 13:6

Talking to God

Now I lay me down and smile.

I'll go to sleep in just a while.

But first I want to talk and sing,

To You, dear Lord, my heavenly king.

♥ ♥ ♥ ♥ ♥

*You, LORD, are all I want!...Even in the
darkest night...I will always look to you, as you stand beside
me and protect me from fear.*

PSALM 16:5,6

51

Night Lights

When the sun goes down at night,
The crickets gather near.
Listen very carefully—
They're chirping! Can you hear?

Watch the sparkling fireflies.
Their tails light up the night.
Flashing, gleaming in the dark,
Oh, what a twinkly sight!

*Let all things praise the name of the LORD because they
were created at his command.*
PSALM 148:5

(Tune: "Jack and Jill")

Look! A blazing, shooting star!
It trails a stream of light.
Streaking through the evening sky,
It disappears from sight.

(Softly and slowly)
Now it's time to close your eyes.
Come nestle down in bed.
Never fear, for God is near
To care for sleepyheads.

You, LORD God, are my protector.
PSALM 7:1

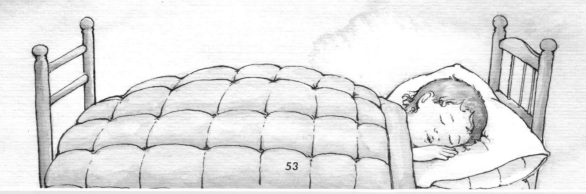

53

A Barnyard
Good Night

When farmer's day is finally done,
The barnyard creatures, every one,
Politely thank him as they say,
"We're grateful for our food today."

❁ ❁ ❁ ❁ ❁

All creatures on earth...come
praise the LORD!
PSALM 148:7

54

"Woof!" barks the dog.
"Oink!" says the hog.
The dove calls, "Coo!"
The cow says, "Moo!"

"Quack!" says the duck,
While hen says, "Cluck!"
The calf says, "Maa!"
The lamb calls, "Baa!"

The pup how-wows,
While cat meows.
The horses neigh,
And donkeys bray.

Creation's Praise

(Tune: "*Camptown Races*")

Let the mountain, hill, and trees,

Praise Him, praise Him.

Caterpillar, bugs, and bees,

Sing praise to God!

CHORUS

Lift up your praise.

Loud voices raise.

Everything on earth below,

Sing praise to God!

❀ ❀ ❀ ❀

Praise the LORD from the earth...all hills...
trees and...creeping things.
PSALM 148:7-10 NKJ

(Softer)

Let the moon and stars of light,

Praise Him, praise Him.

Shine and sparkle in the night,

Beam praise to God!

CHORUS

Whisper your praise.

Soft voices raise.

Stars and moon in heav'n above,

Beam praise to God!

❀ ❀ ❀ ❀

Praise the LORD from the heavens…
Praise Him, sun and moon. Praise Him,
all you stars of light!
PSALM 148:1,3 NKJ

Night Sounds

Have you heard the noises and sounds of the night?
The chirp of the cricket? Cat's purr of delight?
Have you heard the chatter and coo of the dove,
Who quiets her young in the rafters above?

The whispers of nighttime will only be heard
When *you* become still in your "nest" like a bird.
Then you will hear many new sounds that are said
By creatures who wake...after *you* go to bed!

Dawn Sounds

cock-a-doodle-dooooo...

When night time is ending, at just before dawn,
The rooster starts crowing, the cat starts to yawn.
Small birds wake and warble before there's one ray
Of sunshiny beams that begin a new day.

If *you* ever wake in the blackness of night,
Remember that sunrise will bring back the light.
This moment of peace is the best time to pray.
Just ask God to help you and bless you today.

Night Rain

The raindrops fall down
In rhythm and song;
Lean back on your pillow
And sing along.

The leaves whisper welcome,
As breezes blow,
While sweet garden peas
Stretch up leaves and grow.

The chickadees search
For worms in the ground,
Who poke up their heads
And wiggle around.

The daffodil trumpets
Will bloom and sway,
When you wake up to
A bright, shiny day!

*God takes care of his own,
even while they sleep.*
PSALM 127:2

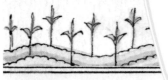

You Are Special

*Children are a blessing and a gift
from the LORD.*

PSALM 127:3

You're special and different, it clearly appears.

Not one other person has your eyes and ears.

God made all your fingers, your nose, and your hair.

You're our special blessing, an answer to prayer.

We're glad that God made *you*,

Our Dearest and Best!

Let's thank God together,

Then lie down to rest.

63

Sing for Joy!

Rejoice in your Maker;
Be glad in your King.
Let's praise God with dancing.
Let's clap hands and sing.

Blow trumpets, crash cymbals;
Let's make up a song.
Be thankful that Jesus
Is good, kind, and strong.

Try humming a song;
Say a prayer in your head.
Then try to calm down
And start heading for bed!

*Praise God with trumpets...tambourines and
dancing...with clashing cymbals.*
PSALM 150:3-6

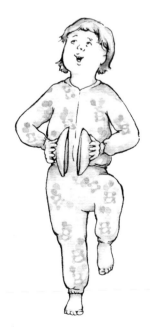

May God Bless You

May God bless your head,

And all your thinking.

May God bless

your eyes,

And all your seeing.

May God bless

your ears,

And all your hearing.

May God bless your mouth,

And all your speaking.

May God bless your heart,

And all your loving.

May God bless you! Amen.

Jesus Loves Children

Jesus said,
*"Let the children come to me! Don't try to stop them.
People who are like these children belong to God's kingdom."*

LUKE 18:16

Jesus cares for all the children,

All the children of the world.

There's no need to cry or fear,

He's alive and always near.

Jesus cares for all the

Children of the world.

(Tune: *"Jesus Loves the Little Children"*)

God will wipe away every tear from their eyes; there shall be no more death, nor sorrow, nor crying. There shall be no more pain.

REVELATION 21:4 NKJ

Jesus made a home in Heaven
For the children of the world.
No more hurt or pain or fears;
He will wipe away your tears.
Jesus' home is for the
Children of the world.

God Made You

We thank and praise God,
As we kiss your dear face,
For helping you grow
In a small secret place.

God formed all the bones
In your arms, legs, and feet,
And holds them together
With skin, soft and sweet.

♥ ♥ ♥ ♥ ♥

*I praise you because of the wonderful way
you created me.*
PSALM 139:14

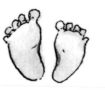

Recipe #2 for Sweet Dreams

*S*hare a time when you felt glad.

Share whatever makes you sad.

Think how Jesus cares for you.

Think about His promise true.

Yawn, relax, and close your eyes,

While I sing sweet lullabies.

The LORD is good. His love...will last forever.
PSALM 100:5

When Hard Times Come

All pain and sickness, hurt and tears,
Last only for a while.

God's loving arms enfold you close.
There's joy ahead, so smile.

Take all your needs to God in prayer.
Then trust, rejoice, and sing.

For God has promised *good* will come
From every hurtful thing!

Put all your troubles in God's hand,
As you lie down to rest.

Enjoy the blessing of your sleep.
God gives you what is best!

* * * * *

We know that God is always at work for
the good of everyone who loves him.
ROMANS 8:28

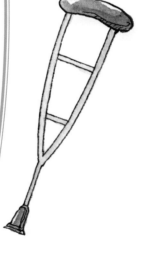

Trust God

(Tune: *"Jesus Loves Me"*)

When in life, things turn out wrong,
Jesus gives my heart a song.
I can trust He'll do what's best.
He'll bring good from all the rest.

CHORUS

Yes, I can trust Him.
Yes, I can trust Him.
Yes, I can trust Him.
God takes good care of me.

The LORD protects his people, and they can come to him in times of trouble.
PSALM 37:39

March to Bed!

(Tune: *"This Old Man"*)

March to bed, one by one.

Every daughter, every son.

With a snuggle-up, Buttercup,
Little Sleepyhead!
Jump into your featherbed!

March to bed, two by two.

Please take off your socks and shoes.

With a snuggle-up, Buttercup,
Little Sleepyhead!
Jump into your featherbed!

The commandment that God has given us is:
"Love God and love each other!"

1 JOHN 4:21

March to bed, three by three.

Hand your dirty clothes to me.

> *With a snuggle-up, Buttercup,*
> *Little Sleepyhead!*
> *Jump into your featherbed!*

March to bed, four by four.

March right to your bedroom door.

> *With a snuggle-up, Buttercup,*
> *Little Sleepyhead!*
> *Jump into your featherbed!*

March to bed, five by five.

Hop and skip—now take a dive.

> *With a snuggle-up, Buttercup,*
> *Little Sleepyhead!*
> *Jump into your featherbed!*

March to bed, six by six
Put away your bag of tricks!
  With a snuggle-up, Buttercup,
  Little Sleepyhead!
  Jump into your featherbed!

March to bed, seven by seven.
No more nighttime up in Heav'n!
  With a snuggle-up, Buttercup,
  Little Sleepyhead!
  Jump into your featherbed!

March to bed, eight by eight.

Don't trip on that roller skate!

> *With a snuggle-up, Buttercup,*
> *Little Sleepyhead!*
> *Jump into your featherbed!*

March to bed, nine by nine.

Brush your teeth; please wait in line.

> *With a snuggle-up, Buttercup,*
> *Little Sleepyhead!*
> *Jump into your featherbed!*

March to bed, ten by ten.

Time to fall asleep—again!

> *With a snuggle-up, Buttercup,*
> *Little Sleepyhead!*
> *Jump into your featherbed!*

Rest in God's Hands

Through puffs of clouds, the twinkling stars
And silver moon are peeping.
Small creatures heading back to home
Are slowly, softly creeping.

The Springtime flowers gently close,
While newborn lambs lay sleeping.
Good night, my Sweet. Rest in God's hands.
They hold you in safe keeping.

♥ ♥ ♥ ♥ ♥

*I am God now and forever. No one can
snatch you from me.*
ISAIAH 43:13

78

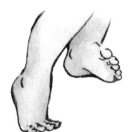

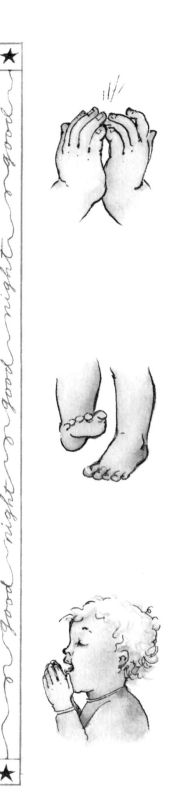

Clap and Kiss

Let me hear your hands go
Clap, clap, clap!
I can hear your fingers
Snap, snap, snap!

Let me hear your feet go
Thump, thump, thump!
I can watch your legs make
One last *jump!*

Let me watch you snuggle
Down in bed,
Fold your hands to pray and
Bow your head.

Let me see your eyes shut—
Close them tight.
Let me hear your prayers,
Then kiss, *"Good night!"*

Night Sights

(Tune: *"I See the Moon"*)

I see the moon, all shiny bright,
Beam down on me in the darkest night.
I pray the moon with silv'ry light
Beams on the child I love.

I see the clouds that float up high,
Turn pink and red in the evening sky.
I pray the clouds that drift on by,
Drift o'er the child I love.

I see the stars; they peek and shine.
God's special lights for the darkest time.
I pray the twinkling star design,
Shines on the child I love.

★ ★ ★ ★ ★

The heavens keep telling the
wonders of God.
PSALM 19:1

I see the owl; the owl secs me,
High from its nest in the old fir tree.
I pray the owl that watches me,
Watches the child I love.

Winter Hushabye

Oh, hushabye, lullaby, rockabye, sleep;

While snowflakes are falling, so gently and deep.

A million bright diamonds lie scattered around.

They sparkle and glitter all over the ground.

The chickadees sleep in their nest, safe and warm.

They don't cry or worry in wintery storm.

For God brings the morning, all shiny and bright,

For you to enjoy when you wake from the night.

♥ ♥ ♥ ♥ ♥

Everything God created is good.
1 TIMOTHY 4:4

Prayer to God

I fold my hands
And bow my head.
You listen from above.

I lift my hands
To thank You for
Your everlasting love.

I close my eyes
To fall asleep.
You keep me safe from harm.

Almighty God,
You hold me close,
Encircled in Your arms.

♥ ♥ ♥ ♥ ♥

The eternal God carries us in his arms.
DEUTERONOMY 33:27

Christmas Evening

Mary gave birth to her first-born son…
and laid him on a bed of hay, because there was no room
for them in the inn.

Luke 2:7

Now if you were there

On that first Christmas night,

And talked to the donkey,

Who stood by the light,

He may have explained,

"I have walked up and down.

This sweet mother rode me to Bethlehem town.

I gently and carefully traveled each road.

Determined and steady, I carried my load."

84

And if you climbed up to the rafters so high

And listened to hear that dear baby's first cry,

The dove may have whispered,

"I'll coo him to sleep,

With soft lullabies as I twitter and peep."

The cow may have mooed,

"Take my trough for His bed,

Let Jesus lie down. Put straw under His head.

I won't use the manger for my meals of hay,

So Jesus can slumber all night and each day."

85

The sheep snuggled close
To the manger of wood.
"My wool makes a warm, comfy blanket
that should
Keep Jesus all cozy and peaceful in sleep.
Cut part of my wool; line the manger so deep."

Now each stable animal, every last one,
Was happy to help Him—
God's dear precious Son.

Serve each other with love.
GALATIANS 5:13

86

Jesus Hears Me

(Tune: *"Jesus Loves Me"*)

Jesus hears me when I pray.

I can talk to Him all day.

I can tell Him when I'm sad.

He will listen when I'm glad.

CHORUS

Yes, Jesus hears me.

Yes, Jesus hears me.

Yes, Jesus hears me.

He listens when I pray.

♥ ♥ ♥ ♥ ♥

Don't worry...pray about everything.
PHILIPPIANS 4:6

Mama's Bedtime Gift

(Tune: *"Hush, Little Baby"*)

Hush, Honey baby, don't you cry.
Mama's going to bake you a cherry pie.

Jesus said,
*"Now I tell you to love each other;
as I have loved you."*
JOHN 15:12

And when that cherry pie is gone,
Mama's going to sing while you hum along.

And when night darkness fills the sky,
Mama's going to catch you a firefly.

And sitting by the flickering light,
Mama's going to kiss your cheek,
"Good night!"

Papa's Bedtime Gift

(Tune: *"Hush, Little Baby"*)

Hush, Honey baby, don't feel blue.

Papa's going to carve you a wooden shoe.

And if that wooden shoe won't fit,

Papa's going to build you a place to sit.

◇　◇　◇　◇　◇

The LORD is good. His love…will last forever.
PSALM 100:5

And if that rocker breaks apart,

Papa's going to mix up a lemon tart.

And when that lemon tart is gone,

Papa's going to strum while you sing along.

And when the banjo's song is done,

Papa's going to rock in the setting sun.

God Thinks About You

*I try to count [God's] thoughts, but they
outnumber the grains of sand on the beach*
PSALM 139:18.

❤   ❤   ❤

Try counting the pebbles
Along every shore.
The thoughts that God thinks of you
Number much more.

So don't fret or worry

When you lie in bed;

God counts every curl

On your dear, precious head.

God helped you and cared for you

During the day.

Let's give God our thanks as we

Kneel down and pray.

★ ★ ★ ★ ★

God cares for you, so turn all your
worries over to him.

1 PETER 5:7

Bedtime Blessing

May the stars
Always twinkle above you.
May the moon
Glow in every dark night.

May sweet dreams
Fill your mind while you're sleeping.
May the Lord
Be your joy and delight.

❀ ❀ ❀ ❀

God loves you and has chosen you.
COLOSSIANS 3:12

94

Jesus Is Coming

(Tune: "Jesus Loves Me")

Jesus promised He will stay

Close beside me every day.

Jesus promised when I die,

That He'll take me home on high.

CHORUS

Jesus is coming.

Jesus is coming.

Jesus is coming

To take me home someday.

Jesus said, *"I am coming soon."*

REVELATION 22:12

95

The Lord's Blessing

May the Lord bless and keep you,
With Love hold you tight.

May the Lord bless and keep you,
And smile with delight.

May the Lord bless and keep you,
'Til dawn's early light.

May the Lord bless and keep you.
I love you! Good night!

The Lord bless you and keep you.
NUMBERS 6:24 NKJ